I0765343

Erika Figula- Ferenc Margitics - Zsuzsa Pauwlik

The Questionnaire on School Bullying

Handbook

The Questionnaire on School Bullying
/handbook/

Written by: Erika Figula PhD., Ferenc Margitics PhD., Zsuzsa Pauwlik PhD.
(figula.erika@nye.hu)
Edited and published by: Ervin K. Kery
(editor@kery.org)

(c) 2019 Figula Erika PhD, Ferenc Margitics PhD., Zsuzsa Pauwlik PhD.

ISBN-13: 9781690814375

All rights reserved.

No part of this book may be reproduced or transmitted in any form without permission from the publisher.
(Email: publishing@kery.org)

2019.

CONTENTS

PREFACE

Our research group established by the Department of Psychology at the College of Nyíregyháza investigates the phenomena of school bullying and harassment. The term 'school bullying' covers behaviour where the aggressive act has no obvious cause (non-reactive aggression).

We set as an objective to elaborate a measuring tool that provides assistance for experts in identifying the different types of violent behaviour and conduct patterns in school praxis, as well as in differentiating within these types.

Our research focuses on the question of what kind of background factors might lie behind the aggressive attitude and behaviour patterns of school bullying among upper school primary school students and high school students (bully, victim, bystander, intervener participant and helper participant).

During our research, we charted those background factors which help to understand the process of the development of bully, victim, participant and bystander behaviour patterns, as well as how they allow the development of various options for preserving effective mental health.

INFORMATION ABOUT THE QUESTIONNAIRE ON SCHOOL BULLYING

The Questionnaire on School Bullying, with its 70 'Hardly ever, Sometimes, Often, Almost always' options, reveals the phenomena of violence and harassment among pupils in everyday school life in terms of five dimensions.

These dimensions are the following:

- ➢ Victim
- ➢ Bully
- ➢ Bystander
- ➢ Intervener participant
- ➢ Helper participant

Except for the Intervener participant, scale each dimension comprises further subscales. (Chart 1.)

Chart 1. Dimensions of the Questionnaire on School Bullying and the subscales of the dimensions

Scales and Subscales of the Questionnaire on School Bullying	Number of items
Victim Scale	**33**
Cognitive Subscale (apperception and assimilation of the insult)	15
Affective Subscale (emotional effect of the insult)	12
Physical reaction Subscale (bodily reaction to the insult)	3
Lack of social support Subscale (refusal to help by the class community)	3
Intervener participant Scale	**3**
Helper participant Scale	**8**
Reconciling interposition Subscale	3
Interposition appealing for help Subscale	2
Affective Subscale (inner tension in relation to the violence)	3

Bystander Scale	**9**
Keeping one's distance Subscale	6
Fear Subscale	3
Bully Scale	**17**
Physical aggression Subscale	4
Verbal aggression Subscale	5
Exclusion Subscale	5
Positive profit Subscale (benefit of the assault)	3

PSYCHOMETRIC CHARACTERISTICS OF THE QUESTIONNAIRE

As for the design of the questionnaire, the first – according to research by Olweus - step was to define the three constituents (victim, bully and bystander) who are measured by the scales.

For the operational definition of the constituents we created various statements (68 statements referring to the victim, 53 to the bully and 40 to the bystander).

This primary questionnaire comprising 161 statements was tested on a post-primary educational sample of 160 young people (80 girls and 80 boys). We checked the distribution of the answers to each statement and the item-remainder correlation of the scales.

During the item analysis we only kept the most reliable statements (44 statements referring to the victim, 23 to the bully and 23 to the bystander).

The reliability indicators of the final version

(scale homogeneity) were tested on a sample of 1365 young people (731 girls and 634 boys).

The distribution of the sample in terms of school types is as follows:

> Post-primary education at elementary schools: 905 people (423 girls and 482 boys)
> Secondary schools: 460 people (308 girls and 152 boys)

The distribution of the sample in terms of places of residence is as follows:

> Nyíregyháza: 401 people
> Budapest: 231 people
> Small town (population below 20,000): 600 people
> Village (population below 5000): 133 people

During the data processing of the Questionnaire on School Bullying, we first implemented the analysis of the principal constituents for each group of questions.

The objective was to identify the principal and sub-dimensions where the structures of the answers entail the least loss of information, those that can be characterized the most adequately in accordance with the real contents structure, and the questions that are of crucial importance in the characterization of each dimension.

During this phase, we endeavoured to have the greatest total variance (at least 40% should be covered by the model) and to eliminate any questions that:

> Reduce the Cronbach-alpha of the subscale they belong to
> Are of lesser importance in the model (communality < 0.25)
> Do not favour adequately the distinctions among the subscales (We attempted to preserve questions that exercise at least twice as much influence in one subscale as in any other).

We only find those subscales suitable for further investigation whose Cronbach-alpha reached 0.7-0.9.
The temporal validity of the scales and subscales was examined for a two week period on a post-primary educational sample of 140 young people (70 girls and 70 boys) (Chart 2).

Chart 2. Reliability Indices of the Questionnaire on School Bullying

Scales and Subscales of the Questionnaire on School Bullying	Cronbach-alfa (n=1365)	Test-retest (n=140)
Victim Scale	0.886	0.83
Cognitive Subscale (apperception and assimilation of the insult)	0.879	0.83
Affective Subscale (emotional effect of the insult)	0.898	0.84
Physical reaction Subscale (bodily reaction to the insult)	0.747	0.81

Lack of social support Subscale (refusal to help by the class community)	0.823	0.88
Intervener participant Scale	0.769	0.79
Helper participant Scale	0.743	0.82
Reconciling interposition Subscale	0.703	0.80
Interposition appealing for help Subscale	0.772	0.81
Affective Subscale (inner tension in relation to the violence)	0.723	0.84

Bystander Scale	0.722	0.80
Keeping one's distance Subscale	0.732	0.81
Fear Subscale	0.716	0.79
Bully Scale	0.796	0.84
Physical aggression Subscale	0.819	0.86
Verbal aggression Subscale	0.841	0.87
Exclusion Subscale	0.765	0.81
Positive profit Subscale (benefit of the assault)	0.754	0.80

In the subsequent part of the research, in the group of questions related to the victim, bystander and bully categories, factor analyses (varimax rotation) were carried out.

During the factor analysis carried out in the case of the victim question group, subscales were arranged into one factor (eigenvalue: 2.714), explaining 69% of the variance (Chart 3).

Chart 3. Structuring of the Victim Subscales of the Questionnaire on School Bullying on the basis of the Factor Analysis

Subscales of Victim Scale	Factor
Cognitive (apperception and assimilation of the insult)	.866
Affective (emotional effect of the insult)	.807
Physical reaction (bodily reaction to the insult)	.446
Shortage of social support (refusal to help by the class community)	.496

During the factor analysis carried out in the case of the bystander question group, subscales were arranged into three factors, explaining 75.4 % of the variance (Chart 4).

Chart 4. Structuring of the Bystander Subscales of the Questionnaire on School Bullying on the basis of the Factor Analysis

Subscales of Bystander Scale	Factors		
	Factor 1	Factor 2	Factor 3
Intervener participant	.842		
Reconciling interposition		.713	
Interposition appealing for help		.786	
Affective (inner tension in relation to the violence)		.548	
Keeping one's distance			.771
Fear			.726

The first factor (eigenvalue: 2.106), which explained 35.6 % of the variance, included the subscales of intervener participant.

The second factor (eigenvalue: 1.824), which explained 26.4 % of the variance, included the reconciling interposition, the interposition appealing for help and the affective subscales.

The third factor (eigenvalue: 1.153), which explained 13.4 % of the variance, contained the subscales of fear and keeping one's distance.

The bystander question group was arranged into three main scales:

> - Intervener Participant Scale equals Intervener Participant Subscale
> - Reconciling interposition, Interposition appealing for help and affective (inner tension in relation to the violence) subscales constitute the Helper Participant Scale.
> - Keeping one's distance and fear constitute the Bystander Scale

During the factor analysis carried out in the case of the bully question group, subscales were arranged into one factor (eigenvalue: 2.468), explaining 62.3 % of the variance (Chart 5).

Chart 5. Structuring of the Bully Subscales of the Questionnaire on School Bullying on the basis of the Factor Analysis

Subscales of Bully Scale	Factor
Physical aggression	.802
Verbal aggression	.878
Exclusion	.643
Positive profit (benefit of the assault)	.664

So the factor which emerged was called the Bully Scale in the questionnaire.

In this way, we arrived at the final number of the statements used in the different groups of questions (33 statements referring to the victim, 17 referring to the bully, 3 to the associative interposition, 8 to the adjuvant interposition, and 9 to the bystander).

STANDARDIZATION OF THE QUESTIONNAIRE

The standardization of the questionnaire was implemented in accordance with the different age groups. During the standardization, we examined the following age groups:

- ➢ 11-12 years: 410 individuals (205 girls and 205 boys)
- ➢ 13-14 years: 446 individuals (205 girls and 241 boys)
- ➢ 15-16 years: 259 individuals (153 girls and 106 boys)
- ➢ 17-19 years: 250 individuals (165 girls and 85 boys)

In the 11-12 year old age group, chart 6 shows the standards of the scales and subscales of Questionnaire on School Bullying.

Chart 6. The age grade from 11 to 12: Standards Relevant to the individual Scale and Sub-scale of the Questionnaire on School Bullying

Scales and Subscales of the Questionnaire on School Bullying	Girls (N=205)		Boys (N=205)	
	Mean Value	Standard Deviation	Mean Value	Standard Deviation
Victim Scale	**16.47**	**13.72**	**16.93**	**13.92**
Cognitive Subscale (apperception and assimilation of the insult)	7.24	7.11	7.97	7.17
Affective Subscale (emotional effect of the insult)	6.86	6.98	5.60	6.87
Physical reaction Subscale (bodily reaction to the insult)	0.64	1.59	1.10	1.94
Lack of social support Subscale (refusal to help by the class community)	1.82	2.16	2.20	2.43
Intervener participant Scale	**0.85**	**1.88**	**2.52**	**2.89**

Helper participant Scale	**9.69**	**5.12**	**7.85**	**5.09**
Reconciling interposition Subscale	4.24	2.58	3.63	2.58
Interposition appealing for help Subscale	2.34	1.92	1.71	1.86
Affective Subscale (inner tension in relation to the violence)	3.13	2.29	2.51	2.30
Bystander Scale	**6.41**	**5.81**	**6.65**	**5.36**
Keeping one's distance Subscale	5.04	4.69	5.49	4.26
Fear Subscale	1.41	1.96	1.20	2.07
Bully Scale	**7.72**	**7.16**	**12.11**	**9.36**
Physical aggression Subscale	1.11	2.09	1.75	2.19
Verbal aggression Subscale	2.14	2.87	3.84	3.88
Exclusion Subscale	3.72	3.14	4.62	3.73

Positive profit Subscale (benefit of the assault)	0.83	1.69	1.94	2.38

In the 13-14 year old age group, chart 7 shows the standards of the scales and subscales of Questionnaire on School Bullying.

Chart 7. The age grade from 13 to 14: Standards Relevant to the individual Scale and Sub-scale of the Questionnaire on School Bullying

Scales and Subscales of the Questionnaire on School Bullying	Girls (N=205)		Boys (N=241)	
	Mean Value	Standard Deviation	Mean Value	Standard Deviation
Victim Scale	**16.08**	**13.00**	**13.88**	**12.51**
Cognitive Subscale (apperception and assimilation of the insult)	6.59	6.77	6.64	6.87
Affective Subscale (emotional effect of the insult)	7.24	6.96	4.32	5.37
Physical reaction Subscale (bodily	0.64	1.31	0.99	1.75

reaction to the insult)				
Lack of social support Subscale (refusal to help by the class community)	1.61	2.13	1.92	2.44
Intervener participant Scale	**0.63**	**1.57**	**2.64**	**2.90**
Helper participant Scale	**9.76**	**5.06**	**7.53**	**5.01**
Reconciling interposition Subscale	4.47	2.55	3.42	2.57
Interposition appealing for help Subscale	1.95	1.94	1.34	1.68
Affective Subscale (inner tension in view of the violence)	3.34	2.36	2.74	2.34
Bystander Scale	**6.17**	**4.38**	**5.98**	**4.62**
Keeping one's distance Subscale	4.91	3.67	5.12	3.971.30

Fear Subscale	1.30	1.84	0.87	1.76
Bully Scale	**6.90**	**6.14**	**9.77**	**7.98**
Physical aggression Subscale	0.59	1.13	1.61	2.30
Verbal aggression Subscale	2.28	2.58	3.39	3.26
Exclusion Subscale	3.33	3.35	3.36	3.34
Positive profit Subscale (benefit of the assault)	0.70	1.46	1.50	1.99

In the 15-16 year old age group, chart 8 shows the standards of the scales and subscales of Questionnaire on School Bullying.

Chart 8. The age grade from 15 to 16: Standards Relevant to the individual Scale and Sub-scale of the Questionnaire on School Bullying

Scales and Subscales of the Questionnaire on School Bullying	Girls (N=153)		Boys (N=106)	
	Mean Value	Standard Deviation	Mean Value	Standard Deviation
Victim Scale	**14.58**	**11.92**	**11.81**	**13.02**
Cognitive Subscale (apperception and assimilation of the insult)	4.85	5.54	4.97	6.00
Affective Subscale (emotional effect of the insult)	7.52	7.07	3.56	5.83
Physical reaction Subscale (bodily reaction to the insult)	0.84	1.36	1.17	1.91
Lack of social support Subscale (refusal to help by the class community)	1.38	1.87	2.11	2.65
Intervener participant Scale	**1.16**	**2.15**	**3.08**	**2.95**
Helper participant	**8.81**	**5.27**	**5.88**	**4.01**

Scale				
Reconciling interposition Subscale	3.95	2.78	3.00	2.55
Interposition appealing for help Subscale	0.93	1.46	0.49	0.92
Affective Subscale (inner tension in relation to the violence)	3.92	2.52	2.37	2.22
Bystander Scale	**5.22**	**4.61**	**4.79**	**4.47**
Keeping one's distance Subscale	4.32	3.79	3.93	3.65
Fear Subscale	0.89	1.62	0.85	1.71
Bully Scale	**7.81**	**7.79**	**10.87**	**8.96**
Physical aggression Subscale	0.79	2.26	1.75	2.53
Verbal aggression Subscale	2.68	3.48	3.89	3.92
Exclusion Subscale	3.46	2.78	3.53	3.55

Positive profit Subscale (benefit of the assault)	0.91	1.65	1.88	2.29

In the 17-19 year old age group, chart 9 shows the standards of the scales and subscales of Questionnaire on School Bullying.

Chart 9. The age grade from 17 to 19: Standards Relevant to the individual Scale and Sub-scale of the Questionnaire on School Bullying

Scales and Subscales of the Questionnaire on School Bullying	Girls (N=165)		Boys (N=85)	
	Mean Value	Standard Deviation	Mean Value	Standard Deviation
Victim Scale	**15.09**	**15.51**	**13.09**	**15.08**
Cognitive Subscale (apperception and assimilation of the insult)	5.04	7.31	6.12	7.93
Affective Subscale (emotional effect of the insult)	7.88	7.83	4.16	5.75

Physical reaction Subscale (bodily reaction to the insult)	1.00	1.94	1.04	2.10
Lack of social support Subscale (refusal to help by the class community)	2.01	2.23	1.74	2.31
Intervener participant Scale	**1.07**	**2.04**	**3.01**	**2.91**
Helper participant Scale	**8.50**	**4.65**	**6.97**	**4.66**
Reconciling interposition Subscale	3.60	2.59	3.67	2.76
Interposition appealing for help Subscale	1.04	1.55	0.66	1.47
Affective Subscale (inner tension in relation to the violence)	3.85	2.54	2.76	2.06

Bystander Scale	**5.37**	**4.88**	**4.75**	**4.83**
Keeping one's distance Subscale	4.22	3.73	4.00	3.95
Fear Subscale	1.14	1.91	0.75	1.41
Bully Scale	**7.36**	**6.92**	**10.41**	**10.29**
Physical aggression Subscale	0.65	1.73	1.74	2.79
Verbal aggression Subscale	2.41	2.79	4.16	3.86
Exclusion Subscale	3.50	3.51	3.16	3.47
Positive profit Subscale (benefit of the assault)	0.84	1.75	1.38	2.24

THE FILLING OUT AND THE EVALUATION OF THE QUESTIONNAIRE

The self-characterising questionnaire can be used in individual and group assessments alike.

In order to fill in the questionnaire in a calm and undisturbed way, it is advisable to conduct the assessment in a noise-free and well-lit room.

If the subject being assessed is unable to fill in the questionnaire due to a disorder related to reading abilities (such as dyslexia), the interviewer may read out the questions and note down the subject's answers.

Answers are recorded on an answer sheet designed for this purpose.

The instructions for the questionnaire:

"In this questionnaire, you will find statements that refer to behaviour which can be experienced during school conflicts, either between you and your peers or

between your peers. Each statement has four answer options:

"almost never", "sometimes", "often", "almost always"

Please read each statement carefully, then mark on the answer sheet the option after each numbered question that you think best describes your behaviour in such situations.

Before finishing, please check if you have given an answer to each statement."

Based on our previous experience, and considering average mental skills, filling out the questionnaire takes about 15—20 minutes.

The first step of the manual assessment of the questionnaire is accumulating the points belonging to each item of the individual dimensions.

The items of the individual dimensions are shown in Chart 10.

Chart 10. The items of the individual dimensions of the School Bullying Questionnaire

Scales and Subscales of the Questionnaire on School Bullying	Number of items
Victim Scale	**1-33**
Cognitive Subscale (apperception and assimilation of the insult)	1, 2, 5, 9, 12, 14, 15, 17, 19, 21, 22, 26, 27, 30, 33
Affective Subscale (emotional effect of the insult)	4, 7, 10, 11, 16, 18, 24, 25, 28, 29, 31, 32
Physical reaction Subscale (bodily reaction to the insult)	6, 13, 20
Lack of social support Subscale (refusal to help by the class community)	3F, 8F, 23F
Intervener participant Scale	**34, 35, 36**
Helper participant Scale	**37-44**
Reconciling interposition Subscale	37, 40, 42
Interposition appealing for help Subscale	38, 43
Affective Subscale (inner tension in view of the violence)	39, 41, 44
Bystander Scale	**45-53**
Keeping one's distance Subscale	45, 46, 48, 49, 51, 52,

Fear Subscale	47, 50, 53
Bully Scale	**54-70**
Physical aggression Subscale	54, 58, 62, 66
Verbal aggression Subscale	55, 59, 63, 67, 68
Exclusion Subscale	56, 60, 64, 69, 70
Positive profit Subscale (benefit of the assault)	57, 61, 65

In the case of the "Intervener Participant" scale, and in the case of the subscales of the other dimensions, grading takes place according to the following scale:

almost never (0), sometimes (1), often (2), almost always (3)

In the case of the "Lack of social support Subscale" of the "Victim Scale", grading is reversed, thus:

almost never (3), sometimes (2), often (1), almost always (0)

The points belonging to the "Victim Scale", "Helper Participant Scale", "Bystander Scale" and "Bully Scale" are the sum of the points of their subscales.

FIELDS OF APPLICATION OF THE QUESTIONNAIRE

The questionnaire may be used effectively primarily in work related to school psychology and behaviour counselling.

The other significant field of application is research.

THE QUESTIONNAIRE ON SCHOOL BULLYING

Name...

Age...

Class...

In this questionnaire, you will find statements that refer to behaviour which can be experienced during school conflicts, either between you and your peers or between your peers. Each statement has four answer options:

0 – almost never, 1 – sometimes, 2 — often, 3 – almost always

Please read each statement carefully, then mark on the answer sheet the option after each numbered question that you think best describes your behaviour in such situations.

1	I am afraid of some of my classmates.	0	1	2	3
2	One of my classmates bullies me.	0	1	2	3
3	My classmates talk to me in breaks.	0	1	2	3
4	If someone bullies me, I feel ashamed in front of the others.	0	1	2	3
5	My classmates call me names.	0	1	2	3
6	If someone bullies me, I kick something or somebody.	0	1	2	3
7	If someone bullies me, I would like to cry.	0	1	2	3
8	My classmates are friendly to me.	0	1	2	3
9	I think I am bullied because I am different from the others.	0	1	2	3
10	If someone bullies me, I have a headache.	0	1	2	3
11	If someone bullies me, I feel exhausted and weak.	0	1	2	3
12	My classmates annoy me and taunt me.	0	1	2	3
13	If someone bullies me, I punch a wall.	0	1	2	3
14	My classmates say nasty words to me.	0	1	2	3
15	I think I am bullied without any reason.	0	1	2	3
16	If someone bullies me, my stomach and my hands shake.	0	1	2	3
17	I think I am bullied because the others like it.	0	1	2	3
18	If someone bullies me, I can hardly fall asleep at night.	0	1	2	3
19	Those who bully me are older than me.	0	1	2	3
20	If someone bullies me, I dash something onto the floor.	0	1	2	3

21	Those who bully me are stronger than me.	0	1	2	3
22	I think I am bullied because I am an outcast.	0	1	2	3
23	My classmates like me.	0	1	2	3
24	If someone bullies me, I feel down.	0	1	2	3
25	If someone bullies me, I feel hurt.	0	1	2	3
26	Those who bully me outnumber me.	0	1	2	3
27	I think I am bullied because the others do not like me.	0	1	2	3
28	If someone bullies me, I feel sorry for myself.	0	1	2	3
29	If someone bullies me, I feel helpless.	0	1	2	3
30	I think I am bullied because I will not hit back.	0	1	2	3
31	If someone bullies me, I feel emotional pain.	0	1	2	3
32	If someone bullies me, I can hardly concentrate in class.	0	1	2	3
33	I think I am bullied because they feel superior to me.	0	1	2	3
34	When my classmates fight, I join them.	0	1	2	3
35	When my classmates fight, I join them because it is a question of honour.	0	1	2	3
36	When my classmates fight, I join them so that they can see I belong with them.	0	1	2	3
37	When my classmates fight, I try to reconcile them.	0	1	2	3
38	When my classmates fight, I seek help from a teacher.	0	1	2	3
39	If I see someone bullied, I feel sorry for him or her.	0	1	2	3

40	When my classmates fight, I try to reconcile them because I feel bad in a hostile environment.	0	1	2	3
41	If I see someone bullied, I become nervous.	0	1	2	3
42	When my classmates fight, I try to reconcile them because I feel sorry for the weak ones.	0	1	2	3
43	When my classmates fight, I seek help from an adult.	0	1	2	3
44	If I see someone bullied, I feel tense.	0	1	2	3
45	When my classmates fight, I will not interfere because I do not care if others are fighting.	0	1	2	3
46	When my classmates fight, I will not interfere because they might inform a teacher and he or she might even punish me.	0	1	2	3
47	If I see someone bullied, I am afraid to speak out.	0	1	2	3
48	When my classmates fight, I will not interfere because my parents might be angry.	0	1	2	3
49	When my classmates fight, I will not interfere because I do not think that interfering in other people's business is the right thing to do.	0	1	2	3
50	When my classmates fight, I will not interfere because I am afraid that I might get beaten up.	0	1	2	3
51	When my classmates fight, I will not interfere because it is none of my business.	0	1	2	3
52	When my classmates fight, I will not interfere because they would not pay attention to me anyway.	0	1	2	3

53	If I see someone bullied I am afraid of being beaten up myself.	0	1	2	3
54	I beat up one or more of my classmates.	0	1	2	3
55	I taunt one or more of my classmates.	0	1	2	3
56	I am not friendly with one or more of my classmates.	0	1	2	3
57	If I bully someone, I feel brave.	0	1	2	3
58	I push one or more of my classmates violently.	0	1	2	3
59	I say rude things to one or more of my classmates.	0	1	2	3
60	I reject one or more of my classmates.	0	1	2	3
61	If I bully someone, the others admire me.	0	1	2	3
62	I pull the hair of one or more of my classmates.	0	1	2	3
63	I tease one or more of my classmates.	0	1	2	3
64	I exclude one or more of my classmates from games.	0	1	2	3
65	If I bully someone, I feel stronger.	0	1	2	3
66	I hit one or more of my classmates.	0	1	2	3
67	I mess around with one or more of my classmates.	0	1	2	3
68	I bully others because they annoy me.	0	1	2	3
69	I will not talk to some of my classmates.	0	1	2	3
70	I will not show my homework to some of my classmates.	0	1	2	3

Before finishing, please check if you have given an answer to each statement.

www.ingramcontent.com/pod-product-compliance
Lightning Source LLC
Chambersburg PA
CBHW051132250726
48655CB00007B/3023